SCHOOL COUNSELOR

BY STEPHANIE FINNE

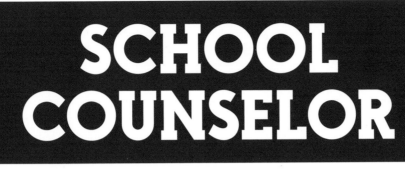

BLUE OWL
BOOKS

TIPS FOR CAREGIVERS

Social and emotional learning (SEL) helps children manage emotions, create and achieve goals, maintain relationships, learn how to feel empathy, and make good decisions. The SEL approach will help children establish positive habits in communication, cooperation, and decision-making. By incorporating SEL in early reading, children will be better equipped to build confidence and foster positive peer networks.

BEFORE READING

Talk to the reader about the different people who help at school.

Discuss: How many helpers do you see at school? Are there people who help with feelings and problems?

AFTER READING

Talk to the reader about school counselors and empathy.

Discuss: How do school counselors help others? What traits do they need to have? How can you show empathy?

SEL GOAL

Some students may struggle with relationships. Help readers build relationship skills by thinking about others. How can they make new friends? What do they need to do to empathize with others? Discuss how learning to do these things can help them build relationships.

TABLE OF CONTENTS

CHAPTER 1

WHAT IS A SCHOOL COUNSELOR?

Edgar's parents are getting divorced. He is having a hard time concentrating in school. A school counselor helps him **cope** with his situation at home. They talk about his emotions. It helps him focus in class.

A school counselor's main goal is to help students. A school counselor can help students develop good study **habits**, make friends, or talk about emotions.

School counselors help students of all ages. There are even school counselors in colleges.

They make sure all students are treated fairly no matter their **ethnicity**, language, or **ability**.

TYPES OF COUNSELORS

School counselors are different from college counselors. How? College counselors help students apply to colleges or find jobs.

Counselors need a four-year college degree and a **master's degree**. Then, they complete several weeks of training with an experienced counselor.

School counselors pass an exam. They also need a **license** for the state they work in. Going through these steps helps them know how to help students.

WHAT DOES IT TAKE?

School counselors care about others. They are **empathetic**. They are good listeners.

CHAPTER 2

WHO DO THEY HELP?

School counselors help any student who needs them. Caleb is new to his school. His counselor shows him around. He introduces Caleb to teachers. He helps him meet new friends.

School counselors can help with **mental health** challenges. How? They visit classrooms to teach lessons about naming emotions. Sometimes they help students find **therapists** who can help them with big problems.

Freddy and his school counselor work on how to cope with being teased. They **role-play**. Freddy practices what to say and do. His counselor helps him practice standing up for himself.

Students can meet with school counselors for **academic** help, too. Audrey has a hard time taking tests. Her counselor helps her plan her time. She and Audrey made a checklist of things to remember. It helps the next time Audrey takes a test.

School counselors also work with small groups. Max and Demanio argue. It causes problems in class. Their school counselor holds a meeting and helps them talk through their problem.

School counselors sometimes meet with groups of students who are going through similar problems. For example, a group might discuss what it is like to have **ADHD**.

CHAPTER 3

HOW DO THEY HELP?

How can you meet with a school counselor? Ask your teacher to help you set up a meeting. Or stop in the counselor's office.

School counselors work with more than students. They also work with teachers and staff. Why? They discuss students' needs. They work together to help students.

School counselors work with families, too. They help students and family members talk to each other. School counselors might suggest other **resources** for a family, such as a support group or a therapist.

School counselors are kind, caring, and empathetic. You can trust them. They want to help!

SCHOOL COUNSELOR OR THERAPIST?

School counselors help solve problems. When a person needs more help, a school counselor might help them find a therapist. Therapists are trained to help dig deeper into a person's troubles.

GOALS AND TOOLS

GROW WITH GOALS

School counselors must be able to empathize with others. Practice empathy by working on these goals.

Goal: Think about someone who is having a hard day. How would you feel in a similar situation?

Goal: Talk to an adult about situations that might be difficult for others. What situations do you find difficult? Talk about what you could do to prepare.

Goal: School counselors work with many different groups of people. Make a list of the different groups of people you talked to today.

TRY THIS!

School counselors teach students ways to deal with stress. One way is positive self-talk. Notice when you are feeling stressed and being hard on yourself. When this happens, think of something nice you would say to your best friend if they were going through something similar. Pretend you are talking to your best friend and tell yourself that.

GLOSSARY

ability
A skill, or the mental or physical power to do something.

academic
Of or relating to school.

ADHD
Short for attention deficit hyperactivity disorder. A set of behaviors that includes restlessness and difficulty concentrating and can interfere with learning.

cope
To deal with something effectively.

empathetic
Able to understand and share the emotions and experiences of another.

ethnicity
A social group that shares a common culture, religion, or language.

habits
Activities and behaviors you do regularly, often without thinking about them.

license
A permit or permission granted by a group to do something.

master's degree
A degree given by a college or university usually after one or two years of additional study following a bachelor's degree.

mental health
Health care that deals with the improvement of mental health.

resources
People, places, or things that can help someone deal with a difficult situation.

role-play
To act out a situation.

therapists
Health-care workers who are trained to treat people dealing with mental or physical issues.

TO LEARN MORE

FACT SURFER

Finding more information is as easy as 1, 2, 3.

1. Go to www.factsurfer.com

2. Enter "**schoolcounselor**" into the search box.

3. Choose your book to see a list of websites.

INDEX

Blue Owl Books are published by Jump!, 5357 Penn Avenue South, Minneapolis, MN 55419, www.jumplibrary.com

Library of Congress Cataloging-in-Publication Data
Names: Finne, Stephanie, author.
Title: School counselor / by Stephanie Finne.
Description: Minneapolis, MN: Jump!, Inc., [2024]
Series: SEL careers | Includes index.
Audience: Ages 7–10
Identifiers: LCCN 2023005508 (print)
LCCN 2023005509 (ebook)
ISBN 9798885246378 (hardcover)
ISBN 9798885246385 (paperback)
ISBN 9798885246392 (ebook)
Subjects: LCSH: Student counselors–Juvenile literature. | Student counselors–Vocational guidance–Juvenile literature. | Educational counseling–Juvenile literature. |
Affective education–Juvenile literature. | Students–Mental health–Juvenile literature.
Classification: LCC LB1027.5 .F54 2024 (print)
LCC LB1027.5 (ebook)
DDC 371.4/22–dc23/eng/20230206
LC record available at https://lccn.loc.gov/2023005508
LC ebook record available at https://lccn.loc.gov/2023005509

Editor: Eliza Leahy
Designer: Molly Ballanger
Content Consultant: Amy Ragland, School Counselor

Photo Credits: SDI Productions/iStock, cover, kali9/iStock, 1, 6–7, 10; Andrey Eremin/Shutterstock, 3; spb2015/Shutterstock, 4; Wavebreakmedia/iStock, 5;
iJeab/Shutterstock, 8–9; Monkey Business Images/Shutterstock, 11, 18; Ground Picture/Shutterstock, 12–13; FatCamera/iStock, 14–15; SeventyFour/iStock, 16–17;
SolStock/iStock, 19; shorrocks/iStock, 20–21.

Printed in the United States of America at Corporate Graphics in North Mankato, Minnesota.